Wendy Lee IrWIN
INNERKNOWLEDGE

Whimsical Recipes

777

7 CHAKRAS · 7 GEMSTONES · 7 SINGING BOWLS

Gotham Books

30 N Gould St.
Ste. 20820, Sheridan, WY 82801
https://gothambooksinc.com/

Phone: 1 (307) 464-7800

© 2024 *Wendy Lee Irwin*. All rights reserved.

No part of this book may be reproduced, stored in a retrieval system, or transmitted by any means without the written permission of the author.

Published by Gotham Books (February 15, 2024)

ISBN: 979-8-88775-859-6 (H)
ISBN: 979-8-88775-857-2 (P)
ISBN: 979-8-88775-858-9 (E)

Because of the dynamic nature of the Internet, any web addresses or links contained in this book may have changed since publication and may no longer be valid.

The views expressed in this work are solely those of the author and do not necessarily reflect the views of the publisher, and the publisher hereby disclaims any responsibility for them.

Wendy Lee IrWIN
INNERKNOWLEDGE

Whimsical Recipes
777

First, I like to thank God, my Rock that provides me with my Angel, guiding me on this path that supplies the tools needed for this accomplishment.
In establishing this published message, I had a thought and wanted to go with that. Creating something, very personal. I believe the world needs! There is an awakening that is happening right now! Not just the people that have been seeking holistic enlightenment, but on a deeper worldwide level!

Whimsical Recipes777

7 CHAKRAS
7 GEMSTONES
7 SINGING BOWLS

These written statements have not been evaluated by the Food & Drug Administration. Furthermore, this is not intended to treat, cure, diagnose, heal anybody or replace doctor-recommended medicine or medical advice. Seek the attention of a qualified physician and a practitioner before using this book, as you may see I use mother may I thought the entire recipes listed because nobody can give you an absolute on a benefit if you indulge in these delicious delectable.

Wendy has captured the value of Fresh Fruits, Vegetables, Gemstones, Astrological Signs, and Tibetan Singing Bowls, arranging them here in her book, Wendy's Whimsical Recipes 777; 7 Chakras, 7 Gemstones, 7 Singing Bowls.

These items are fashioned to provide maximum benefit for the mind, body and spirit. Wendy has designed her book with customized pages formatted for categorizing your personalized zodiac sign with your herbal tea and vegetable source, then matching them with your Chakra and the Hz frequencies of singing bowls. Tapping the universe through these universal allies allow us to create and harmonize the secrets of spirit guide.

What we call "the law of tapping into our own source" is creating our reality at the Quantum level through levels of energy. We also call them vibrations, and if the result is the same, we call them signs; Signs can be altered in time by using the helpful recipes herein. We also include methods that Wendy offers to select clients who find it difficult to stay in prayer (or pray for themselves) by using candle invocations, herbal teas, and flower recipes, in-so-much creating our own internal garden by tilling the soil, planting new seeds and reaping the harvest.

Whimsical Recipes covers wholesome edible products perfectly harmonized with the zodiac signs to circulate the body's fluids for each of the 7 Chakras that are presented.

We are very grateful to share our knowledge that paves a path of wisdom through methods for physical balance and spiritual enlightenment.

When you seek yourself, and truly know that you want to understand about your inner core "spirit" (which is truly who you are), then you - and only you - will open a natural understanding about yourself that no teaching may bring.

Look, if you know you do not function well when you eat shellfish, but teachers are telling you shellfish is how you can reach higher levels of calcium, then it's up to you to seek other ways to achieve your result.

People are noticing a shift in the world. This is the reason why we are compelled to share these recipes with you to enhance your energy levels to achieve your true life's mission. Connect with your power! Allow yourself to grasp a sense of self and express joy in life every day. This is possible for everyone thanks to these tried-and-true cures that are formulated here. Our goal is to share with you a flair of our own whimsical finger print. "Being Whimsical" - being playful, unusual, lighthearted, and a little mischievous in a humorous manner – leads to a light heart that calls a magnificent life, and that I in turn "curse" you with! (Oops, there we are being mischievous!)

Contents

A recollection of making ravioli with my Grandma; A Power House of Wisdom! 1

How Negative Thoughts in Your Head Only Hurt You. 3

Formula for "Little Church in Your Head" 6

Little Church In Your Head 7

How and Why planetary alignment influences our mind, body and spirit. 8

Three Examples (formulated for the purpose of optimal benefits for your mind, body, and spirit) 10

Proceeding with the 12 Zodiac signs: 16

Grocery List 18

Aries formulation "Detox Jump" 19

Aries Recipe "The Detox Jump" 23

Taurus formulation "Here's How Cacao Cow" 25

Taurus Recipe "Here's How Cacao Cow" 29

Gemini formulation "Two of Hearts" 31

Gemini Recipe "Two of Hearts" 35

Cancer formulation "King Crab" 37

Leo formulation "Keep Kool Kitty Kat" 43

Leo Recipe "Keep Kool Kitty Kat" *47*

Virgo formulation "Mermaids Marmalade" *49*

Virgo Recipe "Mermaids Marmalade" *53*

Libra formulation "Fruit of The Vine for Your Venus Mind" *55*

Libra Recipe "Fruit of The Vine for Your Venus Mind" *59*

Scorpio formulation "On with The Show" *61*

Scorpio Recipe "On with The Show" *65*

Sagittarius formulation "Jambalaya to House the Fire" *67*

Sagittarius Recipe "Jambalaya to House the Fire" *71*

Capricorn formulation "Let It Happen Captain" *73*

Capricorns Recipe "Let It Happen Captain" *77*

Aquarius formulation "Super Supper Salad" *79*

Aquarius Recipe "Super Supper Salad" *83*

Pisces formulation "Mighty Try it" *85*

Pisces Recipe "Mighty Tri-it" *89*

Heinrich Rudolf Hertz born 2/22/1857 who was a German Physicist. *91*

CHAKRA CHART: *95*

In my youth I loved digging into the mud and finding Rock's washing them off and bringing them into my room, I always enjoyed planting a seed and (a pit mostly apricots because we had that readily available being a granddaughter of orchard entrepreneurs;) watching them grow that brings me to the 25 acres right here in my own home town of Morgan Hill California a farmers vision to cultivate and supply locals and surrounding areas with gardens fresh an indoor climate controlled seller's market and food hub. I only know that I am very excited when I hear about preserving agriculture, and helping to keep this type of fresh fruit and veggies values alive to thrive and survive.

A recollection of making ravioli with my Grandma;
A Power House of Wisdom!

As a young girl, I remember a few precious moments in time with my grandma:

As I understand, my grandfather was French-Italian, and he was a big man standing five-foot-ten, but his stance appeared over six feet tall. My grandma was four-seven; she was understanding, sweet, a worker bee, always helpful, and she was wise beyond her years. She was the family matriarch as well as to many who met her. I am so grateful to have spent time knowing her as much as I could, yet at the time I felt that I never really scratched the surface of her knowledge. For example, in the 1970s when American Indians came out with silver and turquoise jewelry, there was an invitation to a store opening. It included a presentation with real Indians in their headdress and authentic Indian dance soon followed. As we approached the gathering, my grandma said "I don't care for that," which she said when she knew things about how the world works. She continued "you know Indians are good at cursing. You know back in the olden days the pilgrims (now Americans) stole from them." That's all she said. We then watched the rest of the performance, and mother, grandma, and myself left shortly after that.

Getting back to the relationship she had with food, Grandma would wash the kitchen table and unfold the ravioli dough onto the table. She would follow through with the squared, ziggety-lined rolling pin that makes the imprint on the ravioli dough. Next, she let me scoop the filling out of the bowl outwards and placing the filling towards us and into each of the ravioli pockets of the imprinted dough. If I didn't do it right, she would say, "get out of the way I'll do it," because it was a method she was conveying: scooping the filling away from you and then placing it on the dough is also filling our hearts with love. She would say one word sometimes: "abbondanza" (which means "abundance" in Italian). She saw the bigger picture, that the filling went beyond the food itself and represented the filling of our hearts with abundance, joy, and love. She knew what she wanted for her lineage.

She was amazing like I said; she never told us everything she knew but I remember her just leading by example. That is truly an art, a method that I play every day in the game of life, but now with herbs, singing bowls, and everything I do to stay in the moment. This allows me to walk the awakening path of the universe. Some just let others pave the way, but I say don't be trained by the untrained mind.

Look, of course life may take you off-balance from time to time, if you allow it. This is one of the reasons that I developed a method that I call, "The little church in your head," to put life back into perspective (we'll go more into this later). I believe it is all in God's plan, who created a perfect universe for us to call upon energy to persevere.

At the time, I had a thought about the Indians that she meant something more than using a curse word, and I've thought even deeper on the subject since. Later in the 80s, when I was discovering and keeping logs (intel about my herbal recipes, rocks I would find in my back yard, etc.) I heard about cultures sending energy to lighten the load. I also heard about dark energy (cursing), used to dampen the load. Ten years later, I heard that Ronald Regan invited American Indians into the White House to remove ancestral curses (remember how lovely the 80s were?).

Best Blessings,
Wendy

How Negative Thoughts in Your Head Only Hurt You.

First and foremost, we will address the "little church in your head," because your thoughts are creating who you are; you created who you are by allowing thoughts to digest into Ego Food, and this Ego Food equals positive reinforcement. This gives you a sense of self. That's a lot of power! Now, Ego Poison is the opposite: the negative influence that plays out in your thoughts. It's like a negative movie that plays out in your mind, and one way to shake the negative influence is through problem ownership.

Create a better you from within.

Through our own thoughts we can create Ego Food or Ego Poison; words hold no water until you answer them and breathe life into them. We can use the catch-and-release method by identifying negative words that create Ego Poison, which holds you back and keeps you from your true life's mission. In other words, you can have total control over your decision, and nothing is real until you answer or respond to it. Through catch-and-release we can create karma (which we would like to avoid!) by being drawn into an argument or becoming a sounding board. This is how we can create dharma by making life more active in a flowing way, PAGE) taking the high road through a moral code (such as mercy), becoming a blossom of talents and skills of inner knowledge. You can choose to pick up or leave it; let the ones who are talking smack digest and absorb their own words. You may choose to say, "that's not my method."

Congratulations! You just ducked karma, keeping clean the "little church in your head"

As my grandma would say when we would hear a word of discouragement from an individual: *"the fish stinks from the head."* It means a lot more than an ugly word; just try to say something negative with a smile on your face…it just doesn't work!

Furthermore, it only hurts you. You may notice that person's facial expression turns ugly when speaking, so if this individual keeps it up, then the ugly expression may attach itself to its new home permanently, parking itself on the face.

"Best to say nothing".

You can create a better you by leaving behind things that no longer serve you. Question: Are you speaking from your true source? Are you uplifting yourself and others? Are you happy in your own skin? Are you preaching to the choir? Are you appointing yourself and acting self-righteous? Or are you suffering in silence?
This is how to distract your mind from Ego Poison.

Ego Food is made of 3 Components:

1) *Being well rested*
2) *Eating for energy*
3) *Being vibrant (oxygen)*

Health begins with a relaxed state of mind. "Where ever I am is the place to be happy me". If you are not eating to live for this moment, you may be slowly killing your energy flow.

The third one here is the key, if only you will allow yourself to enjoy your birthright. When you are in a state of enjoyment, and I pray you will reach euphoria, you can begin to reveal the person in your true life's mission. After all God, gave us *you*!

Formula for "Little Church in Your Head"

Designed for the human temperature gauge, the "Little Church in Your Head" is something that I developed. We can visit the "Little Church in Your Head" by using our imagination to visualize where you gather all your information. Some refer to it as the pineal gland, a pea-sized conical of tissue behind the third ventricle of the brain, and which is activated through perception, mood, consciousness, cognition and behavior. Melatonin quiets the body and mind, allowing access to higher levels of consciousness. Picoline (triplane 5, $C_{12}H_{14}N_2O$) and Dimethyltryptamine (DMT) are both said to connect the mind and body. Hormones release into the blood stream that are adrenocorticotropic and stimulate the adrenal gland and also produces a natural steroid, principally cortisol. You might have thought that it is just stress that builds in the stomach (drinking a cup of water does break up cortisol).

LITTLE CHURCH IN YOUR HEAD

A gateway to tune up those wonderful gears of yours into a higher standard of perception, understanding and being understood.

Let's begin by using our attention and intention to your church. Draw a line under your church, about shoulders length. Draw inwards until you reach about 7 inches apart; now you can imagine brackets in the middle of the extended line like so: ._____{_____}_____. we will call this your playground, where you can understand and be understood playing the game of life with an easy flow of energy.

That being said, the left side is cool female energy while the right side is warm male energy, and anything outside your playground is extreme behavior; all the way to the left, outside the boundaries are very cold slow flow of energy, becoming introverted, listless, and depressed when left alone to its own devises. On the right, outside of your boundary line, is a very hot active flow of energy becoming extroverted and overactive at the extreme.

Enjoy your playground, where you are happiest and you have a choice to make decisions! For there is an opportunity at hand. When we are on our game, we get to experience all facets of life at different stages.
Being versatile is key; if one is not versatile, then life becomes flavorless and more stressful. I choose Flavorful.
Wherever I am, it's the place to be happy me!

How and Why planetary alignment influences our mind, body and spirit.

Northern Hemisphere (north of the equator)

Winter begins December 21- ends March 19.

Spring begins March 20- ends June 20.

Summer begins Junes 21- ends September 22.

Fall/Autumn begins September 23 - ends December 20.

Dates may vary due to equinox and solstice dates formulated from the Am-Pm (you may refer to "the old farmer's almanac" founded in 1792).
Let's start with a story that our planetary solar system tells us through patterns that create signs. There are three different aspects: Beginning, Middle, and End. I am referring to Cardinal, Fixed and Mutable qualities. Tap into our own personal power! Cardinal signs: The Beginners, the headliners, setting the stage for the next season workers. Cardinal signs are: Aries, Cancer, Libra and Capricorn. These signs are the motivators and leaders of the band, and they start every season: Aries in Spring, Cancer in Summer, Libra in Autumn and Capricorn in Winter.

Fixed Signs: The Middles, the tireless workers who put in all the content needed, the meat-and-potatoes so to speak. Fixed signs are: Taurus, Leo, Scorpio and Aquarius. These signs hold tight until the task reaches completion. Taurus is the middle of Spring, Leo is the middle of Summer, Scorpio is the middle of Autumn and Aquarius is the middle of Winter.

Mutable Signs complete the script. Being the most flexible, versatile, seer of the bigger picture and conductor of the main performance. Mutable signs are: Gemini, Virgo, Sagittarius and Pisces. These signs mark the End of each season: Gemini being the result of Spring, Virgo the result of Summer, Sagittarius the result of Autumn and Pisces being the result of Winter.

Here are 3 examples of zodiac signs and the influence that the planet plays. We have chosen one Cardinal, one Fixed, and one Mutable sign. The choices were: Earth Virgo for end of Summer; Air Aquarius for middle of Winter; Fire Aries for beginning of Spring. All 12 Recipes are formulated to cover each zodiac sign.

Three Examples (formulated for the purpose of optimal benefits for your mind, body, and spirit)

Every human being is born in a certain season of the year. For example (According to the Zodiac Mutable Sign):

8/23-9/22 is the season of Virgo, which relates to the zodiac wheel planetary alignment and the matched gem-stones that encourage Virgo's healing strength. August 23rd through September 22nd is an earth sign and marks the end of the summer season, being a Mutable sign and the most versatile. Mercury is Virgo's planet and is self-contained with both male and female energies. The Planet Mercury is God of Commerce Communication; being the eight-planet mercury is closest to the sun. Taking this information and formulating this influence, we can derive a detailed worker, a serviceable, personable leader that is creative and spiritual, with a valuable production of active energy. Crystallization forms and patterns link to tiger eye and the solar plexus (also called the navel Chakra), it is the element of the sun that activates the messenger to the belly button, that provides miracles and metamorphosis, intention and intuition. These forces and frequency respond to is 528Hz and is the repairer of your DNA. Tiger Eye is found in Griquatown South Africa and makes a wonderful contender for Virgo because of therapeutic properties related to the head. Intelligence and knowledge represent the winged cap of mercury; this gem stone is at its peak in the half month or, we can just say "season of Mercury, Earth, Virgo." Wendy's formulations show shimmering Tiger Eye is golden-brown with an oxidation of Falcon Eye, iron is the solid when reaching its peak, as if a bird is ready to take flight. The crystallization is a trigonal crystal; this gem is a triangle shape $SiO_2 + FeOOH = 7$ density.

To complement the gem with its herb, we will extend this formulation to the food we eat for the Chakra that is linked to it. Passion flower is chosen because the fruit peaks in late summer and carries healing properties that Virgo needs. The flower blooms from April to November and the fruit can be expected to ripen 80 days after pollination, when it is ready for harvest. This formula works in the season of Virgo. Passion fruit creates an anti-inflammatory that calms the nerves system, making it a great cure for this active mind, in turn providing circulation to the pancreas, liver and gall bladder, decreasing insomnia. Virgo is linked to the solar plexus; the color is yellow, located in the belly button, and is an alert to your body's nervous system, stomach digestion, gall bladder and liver.

Selecting the food that pairs with the ally for the nervous system, for healthy brain tissues and a healthy gut will be the guard dog of this house, so to speak. The focus will be on the B vitamins and Avitamins, to enhance the vibration of the Chakra. Vitamin E is important for antioxidants along with omega-3 fatty acids completing Virgo's Whimsical Recipe for the solar plexus.

My Whimsical Recipe for Virgo's solar plexus:

"Mermaid's Marmalade"
½ cup spinach & swiss chard.
One sweet potato or butternut squash.
Drizzle extra virgin olive oil & blackberry vinaigrette.
3 walnuts. Sprinkle sun seeds.
Cinnamon. Black pepper. Curry powder. Oregano.

Every human being is born in a certain season of the year. For example (According to the Zodiac Fixed Sign):

01/20 - 02/20 is the season of Aquarius and relates to the zodiac wheel, planetary alignment, and the matched gem-stone that encourages Aquarius healing property. January 20th through February 19th is an air sign, being the middle of the season of winter. Being a fixed sign is like being the worker bee.

Aquarius will take the necessary measures to make sure his/her task is satisfied. Uranus and Saturn are both rulers for Aquarius; Uranus is the seventh planet from the sun, representing both female and male energy, and is self-contained. Uranus is the oldest of the Gods and symbolizes freedom and visualizing new possibilities, which are traits of being a revolutionary. Saturn contains male energy and is the God of sowing seeds. Known as Father Time and the father of many Gods, Saturn was the original ruler of Aquarius. Saturn is the sixth planet from the sun, formulating this influence as an industrious leader of innovative thinking, and with an active energy where no task is too small or too large. When seeking out crystallization forms and patterns, Turquoise is linked to the throat Chakra, with light blue to Turquoise green vibrations.

The crystallization shape is triclinic crystal and is rich in copper, with traces of aluminum acetate phosphate (just in case you are wondering!). It is a trace amount and not enough to be toxic. The compound is $CuAl_6\{(OH)_2 / PO_4\}_4 \cdot 4H_2O + Fe$ is found to tame the indifferences between Aquarius and his/her partner. Aquarius is linked to the Throat Chakra and the color is pale blue/green. This Chakra is located in the neck and the element is zinc. The Throat Chakra is the air element, emphasizing self-expression of power, stability and awakening the head cavity. The frequency it responds to is 741 HZ, creating a calm flow on the exhale. Aquarius is an air sign and is affiliated with the circulatory system and oxygen. This is a match, as the Throat Chakra color is blue/green with streaks of gold, same as the ruler planet Uranus, which is pale blue. Zinc is the solid.

Planet Saturn's color is pale gold, and turns color to pale blue at times.

This sign signifies the achievement of mental and physical goals. Gentian for the herbal tea, which may aid in stomach digestion, enhances circulation, is anti-fungal and an antibacterial treatment, when used as proscribed by the herbal seller for 21 days on and 14 days off. Now, for pairing the food that will complement this vibration for a healthy brain and healthy gut for strength and stamina, we will be focusing on a two-part system because of the double dose of physical and mental capacity, as Aquarius has rulers of two planets. It is important to balance the hormone estrogen by snacking on raw pumpkin seeds or raw sunflower seeds, which contain high levels of zinc. This provides improved immunity, prostate, and healthy hormone functions; you're getting your endocrine system working to release the correct hormones to your body throughout the blood stream. This triggers the chemical reaction to our cells.

Raw almonds again high levels of magnesium, which helps with dopamine production.

My Whimsical Recipe for Aquarius' throat Chakra for calm energy flow:

"Super Supper Salad"
½ cup raw swiss chard & bac chow.
One carrot.
Drizzle sesame seed oil. Balsamic vinegar. Pumpkin seeds & Black pepper.
Every human being is born in a certain season of the year. For example (According to the Zodiac Cardinal sign):

Aries is the sign of Fire, the beginner of spring, following the leader as they cheer us on for the beginning of the season (03/21- 04/20). Aries' planetary aliment and its gem-stones encourage healing for Aries. There are four signs that are like themselves most, and Aries is the most self-liked of all the signs. The Ram is ruled by Mars and is Aries' ruler planet; this planet carries male energy and has a thin atmosphere, so it will not support a heat source because Mars carries a thin surface blanket that does not allow harnessing or holding of heat. Mars is an aggressive energy. Its nature is survival, as it runs on animal-like instincts and self-desires. Taking this information and formulating this influence, we have derived at individual traits, supporting a thirst for the outdoors, a desire for working with their hands, and a zest for the open road.

Physical concerns are the ears, nose, and head cavity, as well as the soft tissues from the neck up. This vibration produces an active energy, seeking out crystallization forms and patterns for Aries Gemstone Jasper. Linked to the Root Chakra, this is our contender gemstone, for it brings grounding energy from the earth to the root Chakra. Red Jasper is found in black forest Baden-Wurttemberg, Germany. This gem-stone peaks in the half month, in the season of Mars (Fire, Ram). My deductions show shimmering Jasper reddish-brown with a trigonal shape $SiO_2 + Fe, O, OH, Si = 7$ density. The complement vibration is the gem to its herb, and we will extend this formulation to the food we eat for the Chakra its linked to. Choosing the herb Lobelia (also referred to as American Indian tobacco) may be consumed as a morning drink, chasing away the fogy head about the ears, eyes, and nose. Harvest time is in late summer; only the leaves are used for steeping this tea, but not the plant's roots. Lobelia has grounding aspect for fire but the energy of Virgo, so this herb balances Aries' needs, marks the start of spring, is a cardinal sign, and is the fourth planet from the Sun. Lobelia is a shrub that is bright purple, white, and pinkish in color, and is native to North America. Aries is linked to the Root Chakra; the color is red and located in the middle of your genital and rectum area. It is the earth element, and the releasing of guilt and fear Chakra. The frequencies here to heal is 396 Hz. Being the absorbing-earth-and-fire Chakra, it concerns itself with the intestines, spinal column, bones, and teeth. It picks up active energy as well as stagnate energy, which is why Lobelia tea works as a cure. Now selecting the food that pairs with this type of energy will be focused on free radicals and the remedy to repair damage, releasing toxins from the body; this mainly includes detoxification of the liver and kidneys. This in turn will get the other organs cheering! The focus will be on the Omega: O3 Fatty acids and the alpha-linolenic, O6 for brain development, and O9 that combats cardio diseases, thus completing Aries Whimsical Recipe for the Root Chakra.

My Whimsical Recipe for Aries' head/ears/eyes/nose Root Chakra:
"The Detox Jump"

1 cup of spinach.
3 wedges of Red Beets.
1 Green Apple.
Drizzle Apple Cider Vinegar & Extra Virgin Olive Oil
Sprinkle of Flaxseed.
Turmeric. Oregano. Garlic. Cayenne pepper.

Proceeding with the 12 Zodiac signs:

Birth dates. Months of the year.
Elements: Earth. Water. Wind. Fire.

Zodiac sings are a representative of various patterns formed by stars. Information here is gathered for the purpose of focusing on the influencer.

The influencer is created by our Solar System in three different aspects; that are linked to three different groups the Cardinal; the Mutable; and the Fixed. You will find each Planet is paired with Zodiac and a Greek History Summary from all 12 major Greek God. Zeus, Poseidon, Hera, Demeter, Aphrodite, Athena, Artemis, Apollo, Ares, Hephaestus, Hermes, and either Hestia or Dionysus. Reading Mythical stories that pertains to Star Patterns, called Consolations.

The Tarot Cards are featured here to match each Major Arcana from the deck that represents Aries through Pisces.

Body Concerns: are a list of Relevant Body Parts, that are most concerned with Zodiacs physical body.

Spiritual Concerns: are signs that are out of balance or are a negative trait from ones thought processes.

The Gemstones appeals to each Chakra to Balance the Body's Natural Harmonic Flow.

Whimsical Recipes are the Formulas for your body's chemistry that may need the encouragement to build a better you.

Thank you in advance for using theses Whimsical Recipes, happy that you are playing with fresh fruit and vegetables herbs and tea elixirs. It is so much fun to feel alive every day eating raw produce that may prevent our cells from free radical damage.

Grocery List

Vegetables:
Artichoke. Butternut squash. Cabbage. Carrots. Celery. Mustard Greens. Red Beats. Sweet Potatoes. Spinach. Swiss Chard. Turnips.

Fruits:
Apricots. Avocado. Bananas. Blackberries. Blueberries. Tomatoes. Cranberries. Green Apples. Lemon. Oranges. Papaya. Pineapple. Tangerines.

Herbs/ Spices:
Black pepper. Cinnamon. Curry. Cyan. Garlic. Ginger. Honey. Molasses. Nutmeg Oregano. Parsley. Turmeric. Apple Cider Vinegar. Blackberry Vinaigrette. Nuts. Seeds. Oils. Alkaline water. 100% Unsweetened Cocoa powder. Vinaigrette. Extra Virgin Olive Oil. Sesame Seed Oil. Raw Pumpkin Seeds. Raw Sunflower Seeds. Raw Walnuts. Flax Seeds.

Aries formulation
"Detox Jump"

Birthdays and Months 03/21 through 04/20.
Fire Ram. Cardinal Sign. Planet Mars. Tarot Card Fool.
Body Concerns: Head, Brain, Eyes and Face.
Spiritual Concerns: May enlist false friends for finances.

Root Chakra: Gemstone Jasper: May Harmonize peace with in. Dispel jealousy. Stimulates sexual feelings and fertility.

Third Eye & Throat Chakra: Gemstone Aquamarine: May reduce head cavity inflammation of the soft tissues in the nose, eyes, ears and at necks base

The Greeks matched Aries with the flying Ram that saved Phrixus and Helle, children of Boeotian, King of Athames from being killed by their wicked stepmother, that may have been why Aries is named in Greek legend "One who is of the Golden Fleece".

Aries recipe best matched for planetary vibration about Mars in Fire.

Spinach: Rich in iron supports the immune system functions.

Red Beets: Are high in natural nitrates which are turned into nitric oxide in the body as it may dilate blood vessels. Stimulates the hormones and regulates neurotransmission. May reduce the risk of stroke and heart disease. Because low levels of nitrates may lead to chronic; P.T.S.D.

Green Apple: Pectin Promotes Prebiotics that may prevent cancer growth in the gut by creating healthy bacteria.

Walnuts: Delivers a healthy brain benefit. Helps keep a clean gut and heart health. Improves sperm vitality.

Apple Cider Vinegar: May Prevent Heart Burn; Acid Reflux. Lowers the risk of sugars that are ingested in the pancreatic so that it regulates glucose levels.

Extra Virgin Olive Oil: Loving life in large amounts of antioxidants. Rich in Monounsaturated Fats. Reducer of Stroke Risks. A heart defender of cardio defects. Improves Bone Density and assists in a healthy body weight.

Flaxseed: Can contains compound of 3 fatty acids Omega 3 the alpha-linolenic slow plaque buildup. As in wild salmons ALA. Omega 6 contains crucial compounds of aiding normal development in the brain necessary because the body may not make them on its own. Omega 9 reducing bad LDL; contributes in combatting cardiovascular diseases.

Turmeric: Combats inflammation in the cells. Scientific reports have shown turmeric is a strong anti-inflammatory & antioxidant. This orange-red spice in color helps in Blocking Enzymes that cause many body Inflammations especially in the Brain as well as in the Heart.

Oregano: Aids stomach digestion. Also, an Anti-inflammatory, Antibacterial, Antiviral, and an Antifungal.

Garlic: May fight bacteria fungi in the blood system fighting off viruses, and parasites. Lowers high blood pressure. Controls Hardening of the Arteries. Enhancing Male Fertility. Improving Sexual Dysfunctions; including blocking of E coli.

Cayenne Pepper: Found by many to be a milder spice than other peppers are. Provides multi beneficial plant compounds. 72% vitamin C. 50% of vitamin A. Aids in Vision. An immune system strengthener. Cell protector that improves heart lungs kidney and liver functions. A healthy way to help maintain a healthy weight. This pungent pepper is part of the night shade family.

Aries Recipe
"The Detox Jump"

1 Cup of Spinach.
3 Wedges of Red Beets.
1 Green Apple. Drizzle Apple Cider Vinegar & Extra Virgin Olive Oil. Sprinkle of Flaxseed. Turmeric. Oregano. Garlic. Cayenne pepper.

May incorporate a cup of hot Lobelia herbal tea to sooth inflamed ears, head, and nose, may heal the soft tissues areas about Aries.

Taurus formulation

"Here's How Cacao Cow"

Birthdays and Months 04/21 through 05/20.
Earth Bull. Fixed Sign. Planet Venus. Tarot Card Hierophant.
Body Concerns: Ears, Throat, Neck, Eyes.
Spiritual Concerns: Self-worth what your mind can conceive you can achieve.

Chakra Heart: Gemstone Rhodochrosite: A letter of love & a financial set of values.

Chakra Crown: Gemstone Diamond: May bring clarity of mind. Let the answer come.

Taurus ruler planet is Venus, in Greek Mythology Goddess. Virgin Hestia maternal mother muse a consistence and stable earthy prestress of the home. This lucky lady loved by many she is the Goddess of love, beauty, desires ruler over fertility, and prosperity.

Taurus recipe best suited for this planetary vibration about Venus in Earth.

Blackberries: Ripened in the summer this purple-black in color even found in indigo; helps stomach digestion. It is a supper source for some who dig into this delightful digestive track cleanser. Full of vitamin C and Potassium. Full of Fiber that breaks down toxins and Relieves Inflammation and Infections through the body. Antioxidants which can fight the onset of tumors in the belly area.

Blueberries: Marginally Managed Manganese Minerals that may carry much antibacterial boosters. May prevent tooth infection. The Minerals here are known to improve Alzheimer's and improve cardiovascular health.
A reducer of gastrointestinal symptoms. Ease pressures the urinary track due to on set or from infections.
Boosts immunity support. Anthocyanins in blueberries supports blood circulation and strengthen delicate capillaries in the eyes.

Banana: Rich in nourishing nutrients in pregnant women as it meets baby's development needs. For men it regulates the bromelain hormones of testosterone boosting virility. Improves digestion prevents diseases for better immune health. High in Vitamin B6, fiber, Vitamin C, and Manganese.

Walnuts: Contain lots of polyunsaturated fats. Alpha-linolenic have anti-inflammatory effects in the blood and in the blood vessels.

Extra Virgin Olive Oil & Balsamic Vinegar: improve cholesterol levels & polyphenols. May prevents clogged
arteries; a dynamic duo.

Balsamic Vinaigrette: May help lower cholesterol. Improve Digestion. promotes weight loss. Lower diabetes by lowering the risk of sugars that are ingested in the pancreatic, and regulates the glucose.

Black Pepper: Make way for the King! A producer of red blood cells. Found to regulate heart rate and correct blood pressure issues.

Taurus Recipe
"Here's How Cacao Cow"

½ Cup of Blackberries and Blueberries.
1 Banana.
3 Walnuts.
Drizzle Extra Virgin Olive Oil.
Balsamic Vinegar.
Pinch of Black Pepper.

Herb Golden Seal tea may sooth ears, head inflammation, you may try it as an eye wash as well.

Gemini formulation
"Two of Hearts"

Birthdays and Month 05/21 through 06/20.
Air Twin. Cardinal Sign. Planet Mercury. Tarot Card of Lovers.
Body Concerns: Lungs, Nervous System.
Spiritual Concerns: Over annualizing.

Chakra Throat: Gemstone Blue Sapphire: May bring friends true of heart, soothes the air about you calms communication.

Chakra Sacral: Gemstone Paparazzi: May influence forming long lasting friendships.

Concerning Greek Mythology Castor and Pollux; Identical twins; born from royalty Queen Leda of Sparta and fathered by two men one of which was from King Tyndareus and the other from Polydeuces son of Zeus; said to have made the conception when he disguised him-self as a swan. The same encounter produced Helen of Troy. Tyndareus adopted Polydeuces twins and they became inseparable and known as Dioscuri sons of Zeus.

Gemini recipe best matched for Planetary vibration about Mercury in Air.

Oranges: May keep cells functioning smoothly rich in Zeaxanthin that absorb harmful blue rays. Studies show that Oranges act as a light filter to protect the eye tissues from high light exposer. Preventing many chronic eyes diseases keeping eyes moist in value. As a preventive of premature aging due to over exposure to electronic devices.

Avocado: Makes for a fuller feeling while Increasing Brain Functions rich in Potassium and Vitamin E; Fatty Acids are a building block that create the good fat; that acts as an influencer of energy levels for endurance.

Raw Honey: Healthy Healing benefits Anti-Inflammatory, Antioxidant, and Antibacterial. A natural sugar glucose and fructose plus nutrients boosting enzymes, a living organism that acts as a catalyst to bring about biochemical reaction building the systems value in amino acids. Never heat it up or cool it down best to shelf it; for your convenience. Topically Honey treats burns and scrapes. Orally you may add a little warm tea pot water to drop in the eyes, and in the nose, I know right! If you suffer from sinus infections or hay fever, you may ask your doctor if you can? Try putting the raw honey from your local farmers market in the nose orifice; Researcher say that rinsing with Manuka Honey may Kill Bacteria that cause certain sinus infections;

Lemon: High in Vitamin C. Responsible for weight control, digestive health, and heart health. A reduces of the onset of strokes, and heart disease. A preventor of kidney stones, and anemia. May Boosts Energy as it Builds the Bodies Immunity; If lemon is strong for your stomach find other citric options that are high in Vitamin C.

Pumpkin Seeds: Improve fertility in male and females. Creates a healthy fat for the brain. Loaded with Zinc that helps the immune system, and metabolism functions. Awakens the sense of taste, and smell. Fens off toxins and foreign substances that threaten the body's health.

Parsley: May help blood to clot in addition it aids in bone density. Reducer from serious conditions like diabetes, stroke, and heart disease; and cancers.

Black Pepper: Known as the King of Spices. Responsive to wounds healing. A good source of manganese aids in the process of making red blood cells that regulates heart rate and blood pressure.

Gemini Recipe
"Two of Hearts"

½ Cup of Collard Greens.
One Orange.
One Avocado.
Drizzled Raw Honey & Lemon.
Sprinkle Pumpkin seeds Pinch of Parsley. Pinch of Black Pepper.

Herbal Marjoram tea may aid in subsiding cold and flu symptoms.

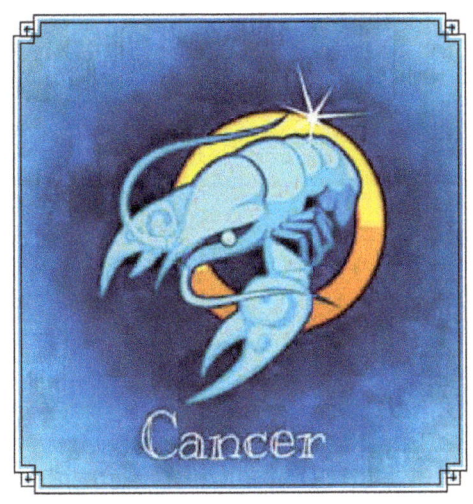

Cancer formulation
"King Crab"

Birth dates and Months 06/21 through 07/22.
Water Crab. Fixed Sign.
Planet Moon. Tarot Card of Chariot.
Body Concerns Breast, Stomach, and all Feminine parts, as well as Hormones.
Spiritual Concerns: you can't side steep this one if you want to finish in first place.

Chakra Heart: Gemstone Emerald: May improve mood swings.

Chakra Sacral: Gemstone Black Moonstone: Feminine Energy a special light for your wishing well at night.

Heart Chakra: Gemstone Ruby: May influence a steady beat of the heart; strengthening the immune system Love dub.

In Greek Mythology; Cancer represents the Moon Goddess Artemis symbolizes an empathetic nurturing mother; Said to have magical powers of healing, and immortality. In a jealous rage Goddess Here, who wanted to distract Hercules; Here formed the constellation of a Giant Crab, that spelled the attack of Hercules. During Hercules 12 labors that was a series of tasks to slay Nemea Lion; Stymphalian Birds. The 9 Headed Serpent; Lernaean Hydra; Capture Cerberus; Cretan Bull; Ceryneian Hind; & Erymanthian Boar; Mares of Diomedes; Fetch the Golden Apple of Hesperides; Obtain Geryon's Cattle and Hippolyta Gridle. Clean Augean Stables all of the above all in one day.

Cancers recipe best matched for planetary vibration about the Moon that influences Water.

Swiss Chard: as a supper food excellent source of Vitamin A, C, K, Magnesium, and Zeaxanthin, Beta-Carotene for Eye Health.

Oranges: Regulates heart and muscle functions. Stabilizing Hypertension.

Apricots: May Strengthens Bones. Promotes Gut Health. Apricots hold Catechin, Quercetin & Chlorogenic acids. Chlorogenic acid may prevent weight gain. Inhibiting development of liver steatosis and block insulin resisting fat lipid accumulation in the liver. Quercetin is a flavonoid with antioxidant properties that may protect against osteoporosis, lung and heart dis- ease. Catechin is a type of metabolite that plays out as an antioxidant.

Tangerine: May Improve Brain Functions. Creates Vibrant Skin. Supports Heart Health. Providing cancer fighting properties. contains 199 milligrams of Potassium, this relaxes the blood vessels and maintains proper blood pressure, as well as protecting the kidneys from stones.

Sesame Seed Oil: protect against Free-radicals. Regulates blood sugars. Relieves stresses, anxiety, and depression. May regenerate hair growth.

Nutmeg: Relieve pain.
Sooths indigestion. Strengthen Cognitive Functions. Detoxifies the body. May reduce insomnia and may prevent leukemia.

Ginger: When consuming this spice to the taste it holds a hot kick, while sweet and spicy and a bit on the pungent side. This spice Improves Nausea, Motion Sickness, Post-Traumatic Stress Disorders; calms Coughs and Common Colds. Fights off Congestion, Infections and the Flu. Relieves Brain, Head, and Stomach Pains.

Cinnamon: Focus is on the Solar plexus that is the stomach area. Takes sugars out of the pancreas.

Cancer Recipe
"King Crab"

½ cup Swiss Chard.
One Orange.
Two Apricots.
Two Tangerines.
3 Walnuts.
Drizzle Sesame Seed Oil.
Dash of ground Nutmeg.
Dash of Ginger.
Cinnamon.
Black pepper.

Licorice Root steeped for tea may be used for combatting hormones of depression will also aid in sugar spikes.

Leo formulation
"Keep Kool Kitty Kat"

Leo Birthdays and Months 07/23 through 08/22
Fire Lion. Fixed Sign. Planet Sun. Tarot Card of Strength.
Body Concerns: Upper Back and Heart.
Spiritual Concerns: Think before you pounce.

Chakra Heart: Gemstone Topaz: Balance affairs of the heart manifest a bold and confident king? Or a mild kitten?

Chakra All: Gemstone Onyx: Creates an awakening in the crown.

In Greek Mythology the Sun was placed in a chariot. Every day God Helios would drive it around. One day Phaethon his son secretly took the chariot along the skyline; that's how the Sun Rise, and Sun Set, was created.

Leos recipe best suited for planetary vibration about masculine Sun in Fire.

Swiss Chard: A supper food that contains 13 individual antioxidants as a daily value: Calcium 8%. Phytonutrients fights free radicals. Magnesium 25%. Potassium 20%. Iron22%. Vitamin E 22%. Copper 32%. Vitamin C 35%. Vitamin A 60%. Vitamin K 477%. Fiber 3.7grams. Protein 3.3grams. Carbs 7 grams.

Collard Greens: Contain high nutrients for bone boosting density. Improving REM sleep that is important for all ages, in Dreaming, Mood, Memories, and Learning Functions for Brain Development.
Enhancing Hair and Skin Health. Fortifies with Electrolyte that may Hydrate the Body. Fortifies the cardiac muscle. Circulates Blood though the Blood Vessels. Soothes the Nerves, Pulsations and Muscle Contractions; Not fueling your tissues properly may result in sprains, strains, stresses you may avoid.

Sunflower Seeds: Are a Multi Mineral suppler for body with Copper, Magnesium, Phosphorous, Selenium, Zinc, Iron, Potassium, Riboflavin, Niacin, so much value in this little seed. Great for skin vitality. Boosts Brain Function. lowers cancers by preventing constipation.

Pumpkin Seeds: Improves Fertility in Males and in Females. Creates a healthy fat for the brain. Zinc helps the Immune System, and metabolism functions. It circulates the sense of taste, and smell. Fens off toxins and foreign substances that threaten the body health.

Nourishing nutrients: Potassium, Riboflavin, Folate, Antioxidants, Flavonoids, and Phenolic acids.

Black Pepper: Is called the King of Spices. It is a flowering vine in the family piperaceae, and cultivated for its fruit. We use it as a dried spice today. The fruit ripens as a drupe; like grapes on the vine. The Black Peppers are dark red and inside is a stone like seed; that is the edible Pepper Corn. They heal wounds quicker than without their use; contains Minerals that Supply Healthy Bones, and Teeth. Reduces Muscle Pain from the onset of Arthritis. Aids in Stomach Digestion.

Walnuts: May reduce the risk of obesity. Improves Brain Function and Heart Health.

Leo Recipe
"Keep Kool Kitty Kat"

1/2 cup Swiss Chard.
1/4 Collard Greens.
5 Walnuts.
Teaspoon of Extra Virgin Olive Oil & Balsamic Vinegar.
Sprinkle Sun Seeds & Pumpkin.
Black Pepper to taste.

Herbal tea Ho-Shou-Wu tea is recommended to clean the blood stream and strengthens the heart.

Virgo formulation
"Mermaids Marmalade"

Birthday and Months 08/23 through 09/22.
Earth Virgin. Mutable Sign.
Planet Mercury. Tarot Card of Hermit.
Body Concerns: Lower intestines.
Spiritual Concerns: You can't poor from an empty glass. Take care of you first.

Chakra Third Eye: Gemstone Blue Sapphire: May regulate the thyroid and let's one see how thing really are.

Chakra Solar Plexus: Gemstone: Tiger eye: Like the fire element in Feng Shui, it brings light to situations. Expands awareness and in leadership roles. Create personal growth; and for the CEO's in developing their people.
Hermes AKA Mercury the son of Zeus and Maia the winged messenger God; Faithful mediator between the realms of the dead and the living, sought in Roman times the planet influence communication and knowledge.

The Virgo Recipe best matches for planetary vibration about Mercury on Earth.

Spinach: Rich in B Vitamin's Provides Fuel to the Brain; and Blood Flow.

Cinnamon: Fantastic Flavors of Flavonoids Reduces Swelling Inflammation in the Gums. Some used it as a Dental Hygiene Practice by some. Protects the stomach against leaky gut; A promotor of healthy gut by influencing Microbiome and Antimicrobial that lessens body bacteria.

Swiss Chard: A supper food that may lower blood pressure. Reduces the amount of oxygen needed during workouts to enhance athlete performance, working together with your system. Building and correcting red blood cells, blood vessels, and the cardiovascular system. Provides proper nerve functions that are essential for Proteins that Maintain Bone Health.
Rich in Vitamin K and Zeaxanthin they work together as an eye filter from harmful high-energy light waves like ultraviolet, as it strengthens the eye tissue. Studies shown that eye vision was bettered when groups indulged in this supper food 3 x per week for many weeks.

Sweet Potato: High in Beta-Carotene, Potassium, & Fiber.

Butternut Squash: Has a Disease Fighting Antioxidant that also promotes weight loss. Protects Against Cancers, Heart Disease, and Mental Decline.

Blackberry Vinaigrette: From age of time remedies:

Coughs. Sore throats. Colds. Sweet and silky to the taste a cleanser of infections in the digestive track.

Walnuts: Have Alpha-Linolenic and Linoleic Acids a wonderful way that keeps blood vessels flowing smoothly for a healthy heart.

Sun seeds: Lowers Cardiovascular Disease, you may find Minerals that support your immune system. Increases the Body's Ability to Fight Viruses.

Extra Virgin Olive Oil: Lowers the bad LDL cholesterol and increases the good HDL. May protect against heart disease combat cancer and alleviate tension in the joints. It Fights Inflammation and Chronic Disease. Oleuropein is the substance that protects LDL the low-density = the bad cholesterol.

Virgo Recipe
"Mermaids Marmalade"

½ Cup spinach & Swiss Chard:
1 Sweet Potato or Butternut Squash.
Drizzle Extra Virgin Olive Oil and Blackberry Vinaigrette.
3 Walnuts; Sprinkle Sun seeds. Cinnamon & Curry. Black Pepper & Oregano.

Herbal tea Passion flower soothes the intestines, pancreas, gallbladder, and head.

Libra formulation
"Fruit of The Vine for Your Venus Mind"

Libra Birthdays and Months 09/23 through 10/23.
Air Balancer. Cardinal Sign.
Plante Venus. Tarot Card Justice.
Body Concerns: Kidney, Lower back, Eyes.
Spiritual Concerns: Over giving compromised is not a promise. Emotionally juggling?

Chakra Navel: Gemstone Smoky Quartz: works with ease to lessen anxiousness and or depression. May bring new appropriate paths.

Chakra Heart: Gemstone Jade: May strengthen the mind. Emotions; and the 5 attributes: Compassion. Courage. Modesty. Justice. and Wisdom.

Aphrodite known in Greek Mythology is depicted as both vengeful, and generous. When an island women Lemnos attracted her anger by refusing her homage, she caused her to stink for punishment; Yet generous a giver of fertility and prosperity. Aphrodite children are beautiful in appearance no matter how Demigod tries to mess them up they automatically become perfect again. Her Roman name is Venus a major member of the pantheon she is the Goddess of love, beauty, desire, and ruler over fertility, and gold.

Libra's Recipe best matched for planetary vibration in Venus Air.
Spinach: for healthy eyes. Flushing out free radicals. Reduces hypertension. Boosts hydration. Curbs appetite. Strengthens the immune system. Assists development in baby. Rich in Vitamins A, C, K, Thiamine B1, Pyridoxine B6, Riboflavin B2, and trace amounts of E.

Papaya: An excellent source of folate. Vital in Vitamin A and Copper. Best to eat with bland foods, if you consume with spicy things you may find irritation in the stomach lining and symptoms of bloating in the digestive track; this can lead to cramping. Best consumed in the morning in place of coffee, or as an evening snack to relax those wonder gears of yours. Aids in quicker response to wound healing. Treats Diabetes. Combats Ageing. Reduces the Risk of Heart Disease, and boots the Immune System.

Pineapple: Promotes Tissue Healing. Fights Inflammation. Aids in digestion relieves arthritis pain. Decreases weight loss; as a great way to help post workouts recovery from sprains. Strengthen Bones, Teeth, and Eyes. Prevents Hypertension and Cancers.

Honey: Sweeter than Sweet! Many enjoy its healing benefits as an Anti-Inflammatory, Antioxidant, and Antibacterial. Never heat it up or cool it down best to shelf it, for your convenience. Topically: It treats burns, scrapes; Orally you may add a little warm tea pot water to drop in eyes, and in the nose, I know right! If you suffer from sinus infections or hay fever you may ask your doctor if you can? Try placing a little of the raw honey liquid mixture from your local farmer's market in the nose; research shows that rinsing with Manuka Honey may Kill Bacteria that Cause Certain Sinus Infections.

Lemon: High in Vitamin C; That is a great reach for weight control & digestive health; It also Reduces the onset of Strokes, and Heart Disease. Prevents Kidney Stones and Anemia. While boosting energy levels.
If you find lemon is strong for you, there are other citrus fruits that may work in a simulated way.

Turmeric: Enhances your over-all mood. Fearlessly Fights Free Radicals. Eases stiff joints, and joint pain. Reduces Inflammation in the Joint, and Improves Flexibility. In larger consistent amounts, people have reported that have bile duct problems should not take Turmeric as it may increase the risk of bleeding in the blood vessels acting in a similar way that Salicylic Acid dose AKA that over the counter Aspirin might; as it increases bruising because it might thin the blood.

Libra Recipe
"Fruit of The Vine for Your Venus Mind"

½ Cup Raw Spinach.
¼ Cup Papaya.
¼ Cup Pineapple.
Raw Honey to drizzle.
Lemon squeeze.
Turmeric to taste.

Herb Chaparral Tea may dissolve tumors. Aids in upper respiratory tract infections due to feeling of unloved, tummy tonic for the naval Chakra.

Scorpio formulation
"On with The Show"

Scorpio Birthdays and Months 10/23 through 11/22

Water Spider. Fixed Sign. Planet Mars; and Pluto. In Tarot Card of Death. Not to fret sometimes cycles have to die to create new life.
Body Concerns: Genitals, Bladder, Rectum.
Spiritual Concerns: Precise planning. Scorpio loves to play, but can give off a sting if they feel compromised.

Chakra Heart: Gemstone Hematite: May aid in Preventing self-centeredness; Allows your beauty to shine through.

Chakra Root: Gemstone Coral: Balances love and jealousy. Jealousy happens when love and hate get mixed together. Restore energy flow that may strengthen and grow new bone growth, teeth and Giving Strength, to Cartilage promoting vitality to promote new life balance.

Pluto means wealth; the winged messenger God Mercury, who freely travels between the worlds of the living, and dead, who spied on Proserpina and informed Jupiter that Pluto was under the rule of the underworld. Jupiter freed Pluto and his siblings from their father's wrath.

Scorpio Recipe best suited for this planetary vibration concerning Mars and Pluto in Water.

Cabbage: One of the oldest vegetables on earth. Rich in Beta-Carotene the Lutein in it balances blood sugar levels. Improves Digestion and Excellent in Vitamins A and K; that may reduce the risk of bone fracturs.

Carrots: One serving provides: 184% vitamin C. Calcium. Iron. Biotin. Vitamin K1. Potassium. Vitamin B6, and Lutein.

Celery: Reduces Inflammation in the Lower Organs. Rich in Folate, and Potassium. Keeps digestive track, cells, and blood vessels working at their best.

Artichoke: Isn't great, here are the 8;

Healthy Benefits: Luteolin. Antioxidants. Folate. Phosphorus. Magnesium. Prebiotics, and Probiotics that Improves the Bodies Immunity and Digestion Functions. Lowers Triglycerides that are the fatty acids that create body fat in humans; the L.D.L. is Low Density Lipoprotein that Transports Fat Molecules into an Unhealthy Water Gain. Now flushing bile acids from the liver results in Cleaning and Rejuvenating the Body's Fluids Filters. Detoxing the Kidneys and Liver.

Extra Virgin Olive Oil: Lowers the bad LDL cholesterol. Increasing the HDL May protect against heart disease. Combats Cancer, and Alleviate Tension in the Joints. Fights Inflammation; and Chronic Diseases. Oleuropein is a substance that protects LDL the bad cholesterol from oxidation high in omega 3 fatty acids that's a double bond and three atoms away from the terminal methyl group in their chemical structure.

Cranberry: Here to Help with Heart Health. Clears up and cleans the urine and urinary track and Protects Against Gastric Ulcers.

Scorpio Recipe
"On with The Show"

½ Cup Cabbage & Carrots.
2 Stocks of Celery.
1 Artichoke.
¼ Cup Cranberries.
Drizzle Extra Virgin Olive Oil and Blackberry Vinaigrette.

Herbal Siberian Ginseng Tea for mental stress may circulate the fluid in your prostate and pituitary gland.

Sagittarius formulation
"Jambalaya to House the Fire"

Sagittarius Birthdays and Months 11/23 through 12/21.
Fire Archer; one with the Horse. Mutable Sign. Planet Jupiter. In Tarot Card the Temperance.
Body Concerns: Thigh Hips.
Spiritual Concerns: Procreation.
Mood swings.

Chakra Heart: Gemstone Lapis: May provide a flow of energy with partnerships to understand, and to be understood.

Chakra Throat: Gemstone Turquoise: May quicken the recovery of injury and or illness. Works as an inflammation reducer.
Jupiter AKA Jove Roman God of weather, heaven, and the sky. Ruler over thunder. Overseeing of all aspects of life. A special proposal Jupiter overthrew Saturn AKA Cronus in Greek Mythology and the Titans self-appointed on protecting Rome's wealth. In light of this task the Gods crowned Jupiter lord of heaven and earth.

Sagittarius Recipe for planetary vibration concerning Jupiter in Fire.

Papaya: Preferred by many to eat on an empty stomach. Detoxifying the body by Encouraging Bowl Movements. Maintaining Stable Sugars in the Pancreas. Best to refrain from the spicy foods, or acid drinks to maintain this wonderful process.

Avocado: Makes for a fuller feeling while Increasing Brain Functions. Rich in Potassium and Vitamin E. Fatty Acids are a building block that creates the good fat.

Balsamic Vinaigrette: May help lower cholesterol. Improve Digestive Health. Promote Weight Loss. Lower Diabetes by lowering the risk of sugars that are ingested in the pancreatic. Regulates Glucose.

Extra Virgin Olive Oil: Loving life in large amounts of antioxidants. Rich in Monounsaturated fats. EVOO may help reduce the risk of strokes. Maybe a Heart Defender of Cardio Defects. Improves Bone Density. May assists in a healthy weight.

Turnip: An Anti-inflammatory. Anti-cancer. Anti-bacterial. This makes them a superfood. Fixing them boiled, steamed, mashed, grated raw, or make a salad or a slaw.

Sun Seeds: A Multi Mineral seed that supplies the body with Copper. Magnesium. Phosphorous. Selenium. Zinc. PAGE) Iron. Potassium. Riboflavin. Niacin. Great for the Skin. Boosts Brain Function. May lower cancers by preventing constipation.

Wheatgerm: May aid in Warding off Heart Disease. A plant base protein. It has the ability to Block the Receptors in the Intestine track from the bad cholesterol.

Sagittarius Recipe
"Jambalaya to House the Fire"

Cup of Papaya.
1 Avocado. 5 Slices of Turnip.
Drizzle Blackberry Vinaigrette.
Raw Sunflower Seeds.
Wheat Germ to taste.

Herbal Oat Straw Tea for calming nervousness and insomnia. The oat straw has a high level of calcium that will strengthen the body's bone density.

Capricorn formulation
"Let It Happen Captain"

Capricorn Birth dates and Months 12/22 through 01/19.
Earth Goatfish. Cardinal Sign.
Planet Saturn. In Tarot Card of Devil is depicted as stubborn; also, a finder of great passions & pleasures to the extent.
Body Concerns; Knees, lower legs.
Spiritual Concerns: Refresh and rejuvenate. Remember water can't penetrate clay foundation.

Chakra Root: Gemstone Onyx: a goal setter for Capricorn. This stone is filled with grace and ease concerning this vibration, it may temper your seriousness, while warding off conflicts.

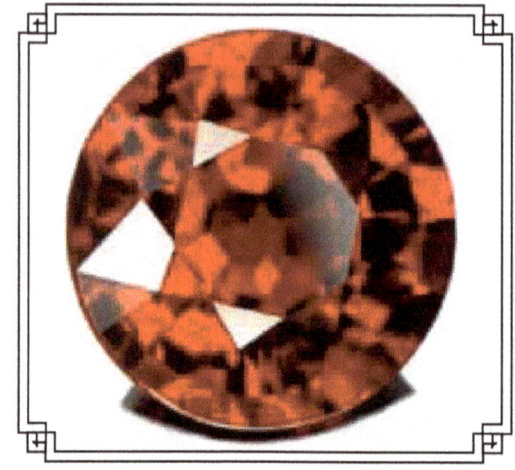

Chakra Heart: Gemstone Moss Agate: May support the heart by alleviating detachments that no longer serve you; redirecting you from bad habits such as over indulging in addictions like gambling, gluttony, grim and grinding thoughts; Working to strengthens the immune system.

Strictly Saturn, Father Time generates abundance. Periodic renewal and liberation Cronus dawn of the ages. Proctor. The seed sower of harvest. After exiled from Olympus by Zeus, he ruled Latium in a joyful way a happy childlike gardener instructor of agriculture said to be the child of Picus. In Roman Saturn, ruled over festivals influencing celebrations of Christmas and the Western world and every new year; Freedom from slaves were given temporary freedoms, and restrictions; In turn this created lighter work load's, in (Latin Saturn dies) was a name plate for Saturn.

Capricorns Recipes best suited for this planetary vibration about Saturn in Earth.

Blackberries: May be a Preventors of Cancers in the Gut and Brain. Bioflavonoid produce anti-inflammatories that Reduce Inflammation's in the Root and Third Eye Chakra.

Blueberries: AKA Supper Food may be Marginally Managed with Manganese Minerals that may carry Antibacterial Boosters that prevent tooth infection. Study's shows a wide margin in Alzheimer, and Cardiovascular health. May Reduces Gastrointestinal Symptoms Ease the Urinary Track from infections. May Boost immunity support. Anthocyanins in blueberries and the 5 benefits: Lower Blood Pressure, prevents Heart Disease, Improve Memory Quickens the Healing of Bumps and Bruises.

Papaya: Potentially Protects the Heart. It tastes sweet and has a soft texture. The seeds are edible as well with a slight bitter to taste at first. They carry a Protective Shield Against Oxidative Stress; And the onset of most Neurodegenerative Conditions. Fights Inflammation. Detoxes the body by encouraging bowl movements. boosts the immune system and maintains stable sugars in the pancreas. Best to refrain from the spicy food or acid drinks to maintain this wonder process.

Walnuts: Have Alpha-Linolenic and Linoleic Acids what a wonderful way to keeps blood vessels healthy.

Capricorns Recipe
"Let It Happen Captain"

Cup of Papaya;
½ Cup Blackberries.
½ Cup Blueberries.
3 Walnuts.
Drizzle Extra Virgin Olive Oil Balsamic Vinegar.

Herbal Guggul Tea is used for a relaxing evening, winding down as an anti-inflammatory and anti-rheumatic.

Aquarius formulation
"Super Supper Salad"

Aquarius Birth dates and
Months 01/20 through 02/19.
Air blowing bubbles into Water. Fixed Sign. Planet Uranus; and Saturn. In Tarot Card of Star.
Body Concerns: Circulatory system.
Spiritual Concerns: Getting balance in relations with others.

Chakra Solar Plexus: Gemstone Jade: May aid in understanding and appreciation of life.

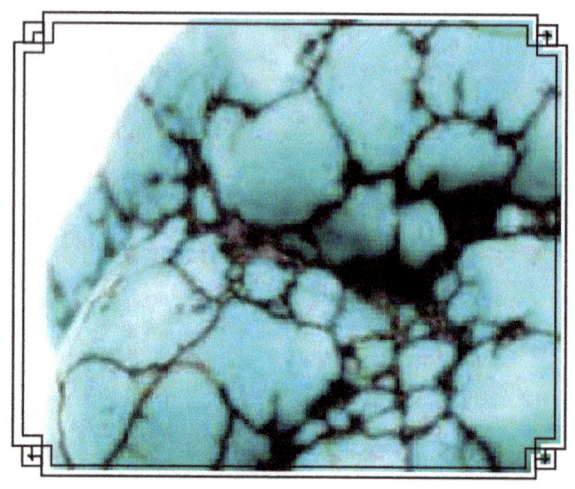

Chakra Throat: Gemstone Aquamarine: May obtain freedoms in narrowing situations; may bring about unity in family, and in business.

Chakra Throat: Gemstone Turquoise: May Turn the attention and intention of the mind on partnerships.

Uranus is all about freedoms and liberties. In Greek Mythology he is perceived as heaven and the sky. Uranus creates freedoms dominated by the light of the sun and powered by Mars. Son of Gaea; Gaea created him without help. Uranus was the first symbol of maleness a circle with an arrow pointing away from it, it is the universal symbol of male. Then Uranus became her husband and together they had a partnership that included the first generation of 12 of the Titans. While the counter planet is Saturn known as the seed sower.

Aquarius Recipe best matched for this planetary vibration of Saturn and Uranus in Air

Extra Virgin Olive Oil: Contains Hydroxytyrosol and Oleocanthal; Translation Antioxidant lowers the bad LDL cholesterol and increases the HDL. HDL Supports Memory, and Brain Function sets you up for a good foundation greasing those wonderful gears of yours. Combats Pain in the Joints, Boost Bone Health by Strengthen the Skeletor Frame, as Anti-Inflammatory to the Neuroprotective also has Antimicrobial properties. EVOO is proven to provide cardiovascular endurance. Aids in cognitive behavior.

Swiss Chard: A supper food may lower blood pressure. Reduces the amount of oxygen needed during workouts; Enhances the Athlete Performance by working together with your system in Building Correct Red Blood Cells. Blood Vessels. Cardiovascular and Nerve Functions that are essential for proteins. High in fiber it is a great way to detox the body.

Bok Choy: Builds up endurance that feeds fuel for the muscles. Consumed cooked or raw Contains Critical Nutrients. And found to be a Reducer of many Chronic Diseases. Focused on Vitamins C, K, A. One cup contains 140% of the daily consumption of this green leafy and white stock veggie. Choy contains more Vitamin C and A than spinach does.

Turnip: A power proctor from breast to prostate cancers; Creating Lutein for the eyes. You may find the Fiber in them Prevents Constipation, and Regular Adequate Bowel Movements; Crucial for Releasing Toxins through the Bile, and Stools. Promotes good healthy digestion for the gut.

Pumpkin seeds: Contain Zinc that helps the system fight bacteria. Relaxes the Muscle Tissue and Heals Wounds. A cell protector from diseases that cause damage.

Aquarius Recipe
"Super Supper Salad"

½ Cup Raw Swiss Chard & Bac Chow.
3 Turnip slices.
1 Carrot.
Drizzle Sesame Seed Oil.
Balsamic Vinegar.
Pumpkin Seeds.
Dash of Black Pepper.

Herb Gentian may strengthen the whole circulation system.

Pisces formulation
"Mighty Try it"

Pisces Birthdays and Months 02/20 through 03/20.
Water two fish swimming. Mutual Sign. Planet Neptune. In Tarot Card Moon.
Body Concerns: Feet.
Spiritual Concerns: Feelings of hurt affairs of the heart.

Chakra Third Eye: Gemstone Amethyst: May balances love, and expressing fish feelings.

Chakra Solar Plexus: Gemstone Jade: May bring Wisdom, Love, Harmony, and Trust.

In Greek Mythology Neptune was the Roman God of the fresh water, by 399bce was positions by the Greeks as Poseidon; at that time became owner of the sea. One path of Juno Jupiter said she conspired with Hera and Minerva Athena to over throw him and put him in chains and placing him in the sea for disobedience. Poseidon takes after the form of a horse as Neptune's Equester, he was recognized as a God of horses and horsemanship, that became entertainment for the ancient Romans considered the God of Earthquakes when he waved and struck his mighty trident he caused the erudition of many sea rocks that created new foundations in ancient Athens. 14 names of Neptune and his 14 moons are Naiad, Thalassa, Despina, Galatea, Larissa, S/2004 n1, Proteus, Triton, Nereid, Halimede, Sao, Laomedeia; Psamathe; & Neso.

Pisces Recipe best matched for planetary vibration about Neptune in Water.

Mustard Green: known to have nourishing nutrients, can lower cholesterol levels, has chemicals that assist in the binding of bile acids in the digestive track. Chlorophyll is beneficial for detoxification. Vitamin B slows the process of brain decline; Protecting your skin to note many minerals like magnesium; High in Vitamin K and contain oxalates that thins the blood flow in large amounts may over agitate the kidneys if eaten in large amounts. This may also contribute to kidneys stones if consumed every day for long periods.

Sweet Potato: Vital in Vitamin A that supports good vision. Vitamin E supports scalp and hair luster. A natural antioxidant preventing free radicals, outside pollutants, protecting against the ageing cycle, and the unfocused brain. High in fiber it promotes a healthy gut.

Spinach: Rich in Carotenoids that is the pigment in the vegetable, known to quench singlet oxygen. A strong antioxidant activity that may reduce the risks of cancer. Vitamin C, B, and B12, calms the Vega Nerve. Allowing the provision of energy to fuel the brain that encourages blood flow. Contains Vitamin K, Folic acid, and Iron. Cinnamon: Takes care of stomach digestion. that is the solar plexus chakra area. It takes sugars out of the pancreas.

Extra Virgin Olive Oil: Lowers the bad LDL cholesterol and increases the HDL. May protect against heart disease combat cancer and alleviate tension in the joints. Fights Inflammation and Chronic Disease. Oleuropein is a substance that protects LDL bad cholesterol from oxidation. High in Omega 3 fatty acids; a double bond three atoms away from the terminal methyl group that are in their chemical structure. It may build and maintains a healthy body.

Molasses: Blackstrap is a nutritious byproduct of sugarcane production, used my many who want thicker hair. You may find the enzymes in it that nourishes the scalp. You may have found in many hair products have it in them to promote hair growth. Relieves Constipation.

Pisces Recipe
"Mighty Tri-it"

½ Cup Mustard Greens.
½ Cup Spinach.
1 Steamed Sweet Potato.
Drizzle Molasses and Extra Virgin Olive Oil. Cinnamon to taste.

Herbal Juniper Berry Tea, for the digestion track you may reduce the intake of alcohol or stop for this time period.

Heinrich Rudolf Hertz born 2/22/1857 *who was a German Physicist.*

Hertz (Hz) is the derived unit of frequency, in the international system of units, (SI), and is defined as one cycle per second Hertz was the first person who provided proof of existence of electromagnetic waves sound that creates energy flow or the movement of bodily fluids.

Here I have shown 7 of basic body Chakra points, Frequencies, Colors, and the Gemstone's that I have linked to sound therapy by focusing on solfeggio frequencies that call out each of the 7 Chakras, in order to harmonize balance and energies.
Concerning the body fluids for each zodiac sign. I am presenting this special whimsical flare that formulates a direct path to the Chakras. The elements, and the gem; that may create a pattern for best result in "Building A Better You" with energy flow.

Root is the Chakra; Earth element releasing guilt and fear. Frequencies = 396Hz
Root frequencies start from 228Hz - 456-Hz - 912Hz. Red Jasper is the gem.

Sacral is the Chakra; Water element releasing ties of situations, it turns the tide, creating change clears negative thought that can hold you back and keep you from your true life's mission. Frequencies = 417Hz Sacral frequencies start from 303Hz - 606Hz - 1212Hz. Black moon stone is the gem.

Solar plexus is the Chakra; Earth/Fire element releasing suppressed connection with others imbalanced as fiery rage Frequencies= 528Hz belly button frequencies start from 182Hz - 364Hz - 728Hz. Tiger eye is the gem.

Heart is the Chakra; Air/fluid element releasing heart ache and suppressed emotions, awareness detaching from one's own circumvent awareness. Frequencies= 639Hz frequencies start from 128Hz - 256Hz - 512Hz. Jade is the gem.

Throat is the Chakra; Air/Either element governs the thyroid influence hearing, releasing force of air, an overly expression of air in the head cavity Frequencies= 741Hz is the balance frequency responding to calm the exhaling of air. Frequencies start from 192Hz - 384Hz 768Hz. Turquoise is the gem.

Third eye is the Chakra; light element gives the ability to see what takes shape, or the blocked energy here that needs to be harmonized. Frequency= 852Hz raises and encourages spiritual sight, higher mind, frequencies start from 114Hz - 288Hz - 576Hz. Indigo Sapphire is the gem.

Crown is the Chakra; Pure Spiritual light space and ether is the element, if this channel is dim than you feel like a dark cloud is over your head, you may ignite your fire with the Frequency= 963Hz it may connect you to enlightenment this is away about yourself that feels the high light energy of spirit with you. In this vibration it is attached to time periods, past life's, present awareness and future values that are gathered here for transportation. The spirit world frequencies start from 216Hz - 432Hz - 864Hz. Lapis is the gem.

Best Gemstone list for each of the zodiac sings concerning the crown Chakra from my work shop "Building A Better You".
Onyx = Capricorn. Turquoise= Aquarius. Amethyst= Pisces. Aquamarine= Aries. Diamond= Taurus. Sapphire= Gemini. Emerald = Cancer. Onyx = Leo. Sapphire = Virgo. Jade= Libra. Hematite = Scorpio. Lapis = Sagittarius.
Now go out and be the light.

7 crystal singing bowls
c to b low to high tones
color and formation of Chakras
Let's create energy flow

C = 1st Red Root, 4 petal Chakra form.

D = 2nd Orange Sacral, 6 petal Chakra form.

E = 3rd Yellow Solar Plexus, 10 petal Chakra form.

F = 4th Green Heart, 12 petal Chakras from.

G = 5th Blue Throat, 16 petal Chakra form.

A = 6th Violet Eye, 2 petal Chakra form.

B = 7th White and Gold Crown, 1000 petal

CHAKRA CHART:

(1) Root (RED) and is located in the middle of your genital and rectum area it is an earth absorbing energy and it concerns its self with the formation of blood cells, intestines, prostate, bones, teeth, nails, and spinal column.

(2) Sacral (ORANGE) and is located above the pubic hair line area it is a flowing energy and it concerns its self with circulating fluids in sweat, tears, urine, sperm, ovulation, and blood.

(3) Solar Plexus (YELLOW) this is the belly button location and it is the alerting zone concerning itself with your bodies nervous system, stomach digestive, gall bladder and liver.

(4) Heart (GREEN & PINK) this is the Heart located between and above your two breasts, concerns its self with circulating the immune system and a call for love.

(5) Throat (BLUE/GREEN) and is located at the base of the neck, it concerns about the thyroid gland, ears eyes nose and throat, and throat functions.

(6) Third Eye (BLUE/PURPLE) located on the forehead between the eyes its concerns are all about understanding, intuitive thinking, perception.

(7) Crown (PURPLE/WHITE) located on top of your head it concerns are with developing and processing high levels of energy for new thinking or enlightenment.

Many problems in the home occur by having negative energy that can hold you back and keep you from your true life's mission.

The 9 Gua's:

Presented here are easy to follow along with this map that identifies the different sectors in your house that represents different body parts.
illustrations of the Bagua to Feng-Shui the mind and body for optimal benefits.

1 through 9 starting counter clock wise
The Bagua is an octagon shape, each side is called a Gua here we will be using this example that represents feng-shui for the Mind, Body, and Spirit; It carries a Number, Color, an Element, Body part, and the Shapes name. Just like the human body contain elements of Fire, Metal, Water, Wood, Earth. Here is the formula list for guidance. Dressing in these colors as needed may attract more energy to the desired body part that may bring your attention and intention to life.

1 Red; Fame; Fire; Reputation; Body part Eye.
2 Pink; White; & Red; Relations of Love; Body Organ Heart.
3 Yellow; Creativity; Childlike; Metal; shape Round; Body part Mouth.
5 Black; White; Gray; & Silver; Helpful People; Travel; Body part Head.
6 Black; White; Water; Career; Body part Ear.
7 Black; Green; & Blue; Wisdom; Knowledge; Body part Hand.
4 Green; Family; Income; Body part Foot.
9 Orange; Health; Earth; Sacral; Stomach and the Entire Body.

In conclusion of this publication is provided a reference guide for a fun Feng-Shui for the mind body and spirit.

My hope is today you enjoyed the showcase that links fresh fruits, vegetables, gemstones, and singing bowels; that when used together create a force field of energy flow.
I pray I was able to captivate you in establishing each and every value here in matching your zodiac sign to each of them.
The true you that God made you to be. These methods are here to "Build A Better You".
Transform your daily stress into power points.
Stimulate your world and focus on you.
subsequently how you rise above. Interpret and present the best you because how you do makes or breaks values.

Best Blessing
Wendy Lee IrWIN.

Gotham web site that was created for Wendy

IINNERKNOWLEDGE.COM

www.ingramcontent.com/pod-product-compliance
Lightning Source LLC
LaVergne TN
LVHW070532070526
838199LV00075B/6764